WHEN

A Woman

LOVES A WOMAN

A MEMOIR

BY KOURTNEY CARTER

Glover Lane Press
Publishers Since January 2000
Sherman Oaks, CA 91403
www.gloverlanepress.webs.com

When A Woman Loves A Woman; A Memoir
by Kourtney Carter

Copyright 2014 by Kourtney Carter

ISBN: 978-0692279540

Edited by Ifalade Ta'Shia Asanti

Cover Photography by Ryan Zimmerman-Lead Photographer
Pantechne Studios 904.463.0546
Email: Ryan@pantechnestudios.com

Cover Design by Azaan Kamau

The Mission of Glover Lane Press is to Uplift, Empower, Elevate the Masses and Provide American Jobs. Every book published by Glover Lane Press and it's many imprints, is printed and manufactured in the United States of America, ensuring and maintaining American employment.

Dedication

I would like to dedicate
When A Woman Loves A Woman
to the Universe for never ceasing to remind me
that I was meant for so much more.

Acknowledgements

To my Brother Jalen Powell, my life truly changed the day you move in with me seeing you start your journey as a man is a gift and blessing I will forever cherish.

To my family for giving me a great childhood that I wouldn't trade for anything. To my beautiful mothers, June Kirby and LaTonya Carter. Mrs. Kirby ... Mom the best gift I could have ever been given was having you as my mother your love is gentle and it is kind.

Mrs. Carter ... Mom, your words of wisdom resonate in me and the way God moves in you is truly remarkable. To my Dad, So full of wisdom, inspiration, motivation and guidance. I have found myself numerous of times rereading something you have sent me to encourage myself when I have felt down not knowing what to do next.

At times I feel you know me better than I know myself. To everything I went through to help me write this book I am so grateful and happy I had those lessons......

Contents

Chapter 1-In The Beginning

Our family traditions started decades before I was born. They began in a wooden house located right off the highway. A place where chickens roamed in the backyard and a "Spodie" red caddy sat in the drive way.

Growing up was life in full effect. There was always family around. When we got together the house would be filled with loud talking, food and love. The Children hung out in one room and the adults in the other. We always sang and played games before we ate. Other family members strolled in at the last minute. They were well known for their lateness so it wasn't a shock when they arrived hours past the start time of a gathering.

I had school during the day. Afterwards I was out balling with the fellas and attending church activities. Time with the family prevailed despite my demanding schedule. Family supported us in the activities we were involved in. Band, basketball, singing in the choir, ushering— we were always doing something.

My experiences in learning about the opposite sex were different from the people around me. Both my family and extended family had begun to see me. I didn't carry myself like other girls. They began to have conversations. I heard but didn't hear.

Even as a young girl I felt drawn to female energy. That manifested as kidplay i.e. *my sand castle is better than yours* conversations. I also felt a magnetic pull to my male classmate's athletic side. My boy friends would chant, "girls are nasty," while admiring their long, pretty hair. My tomboyish ways and my preference of hanging out with the guys—later I would completely understand why my caregivers were concerned about who I was becoming.   Some said it was just a phase. Others knew my secret. Some of my relatives flat out denied or refused to believe who they and I knew I was.

The truth was, women woke me up. Men not so much. Despite my recognizing the difference in how I related to members of the same gender, there was a debate going on in my mind. I tried to convince myself that I wasn't who I was. Confused, thinking with the mind of a child, I tried to act like what I felt wasn't real.

It wasn't until it was spoken to me by a relative did I have even an inkling of who I was. Even then I had no knowledge of what those words meant. I responded to it through a connection to something deep in me. It was physical, pure feelings. That was when the prayers started.

It wouldn't hit me until I was older and in full knowledge of the meaning of those words. All I could utter from my mouth was *wow*. In the stillness and silence of my room, I picked up the phone to call a close friend. I thought maybe she understood who and what I was...

10

Chapter 2

I've always been proud to be from a family that has a strong foundation, a strong bloodline and unshakable faith. Going to church was mandatory until you felt that you were grown enough to make your own decisions but even then the standard still stood that you better give God your time on Sunday morning. Even if it wasn't stated, the principles we were raised on were expected to be observed even after we became adults. And as expected, my family's mandatory religious practices have continued through the generations.

I did as I was taught because being disobedient wasn't tolerated in my family's eyes. I was told defiance definitely wasn't something God put up with. I was warned that you could cut your days short by not giving God His time. It was a terrifying thought for a young child....

Between His love and His wrath, at times it was hard to discern what God felt for me. This caused me to digress in my spiritual development until I began to experience the world and the fullness of its wonders.

My innocent childhood games grew up. They turned into *touch and feel, I like you, you like me, lets hunch* until one of us liked someone else. I figured all kids went through multiple boy or girlfriends between pre-K and fourth grade. But my attraction to girls was not changing or going away, it was growing. I tried to reconcile it in my head but without someone to talk to, someone to help me make sense of it, it was hard to understand.

Chapter 3

I met her on some *young shit*. I say young shit because we were innocent and knew little about the world. We both felt guilty. We thought we were born of sin because of what we'd been taught in church. Being Christian or being Baptist that is—church was not only what we did but who we were.

We went to church conventions. Churches from our area and from other states came together for these huge gatherings. Church conventions were the best time to go to church. You got to see the rest of your friends from different churches, stay in a hotel and get in the pool. You could also hook up with somebody but you'd probably only be with them for a couple weeks. You wouldn't see each other until the districts came together again on the fifth Sunday.

We made it difficult for the teachers and directors leading us at the convention. During rehearsals we would be talking, writing letters to each other and distracting the ones who were paying attention. When it was time to sing a specific section of a song, we had no idea where we were. It really drove the teachers crazy which made us happy.

During the convention we combined districts to create a huge mass choir. We'd stay in rehearsal for what seemed like forever though in reality it was only an hour. Thoughts of food and getting in the pool were on our minds. We couldn't wait to get back to the hotel.

My first Girlfriend...*HER*, she was a talker. She was beautiful and had long luxurious hair. She mingled among us like the social butterfly she was. I gazed longingly at her from afar.

She introduced herself to me. I was a little nervous at first but we hit it off with ease. It was as if we had known each other prior to our encounter. The initial connection was friendship. Later I realized that the friendship thing may've been a cover....

What I was feeling was a mixture of familiar and unfamiliar but I proceeded to go with the flow of the experience. I found myself naturally flirting with this girl. Her smile indicated the acceptance of my innocent play. A slightly familiar feeling came over me. My curiosity peaked. The rest was history.

We became very close. To compensate for the distance between us we spent hours on the phone. There wasn't a moment or day that went by I didn't hear her voice.

There's one conversation that changed the course of our lives. It started off with her usual,

"Hello. What cha' doing?" I answered with my typical explanation of how my day went—how I was just chilling, watching TV, talking to her. Somehow, sex became the topic of discussion. How? I still can't recall to this day. But between the on and off flirting it came up and flowed smoother than butter spread on bread.

What I do remember is, whatever she said first, I replied with words you're not supposed to say to another woman. She played into what I said with her own comments.

That's how it all began. My *journey to heaven* I call it. Where the streets are paved with gold, milk and honey flow. Where I met God at His front door.

They say heaven rejoices when a sinner gives his life to Christ. Your name goes in the book of life. It's a done deal! You're going to heaven first class, maybe. Christians are told to repent for the time is approaching. They say Jesus is coming back for his people—I was determined not to get left behind.

Whenever I think about that experience, the song, *Get Your House in Order,* comes to mind. One of the sisters at my childhood church sang that song so well. I loved to sing at church. Singing was the best part of church if you asked me. It spoke to my soul. When I was a kid, it was singing that led me to give my life to Christ. My family took great pride in the ministry of music for the Lord.

After I got baptized, I sat on the front row of the Choir stand on the Sundays when the youth would render the service. I remember sitting in a brown fold up chair. There were two that they placed right in front of the pews. I sat in the left one and the young lady I was baptized with sat on the right. We were asked our names and why we came up to the altar. When you're young it seems like you understand yourself better than you do in your adult years. I guess because you haven't been exposed too much as of yet.

We recited the words the pastor asked us to say. It was a simple prayer to receive Christ in your life. Afterwards we got to choose a Deacon who'd watch over us. I chose Mr. Joe, one of the coolest, smoothest, great singers I knew. He was the Choir director and held other titles as well. That was a great day at church and I still remember how I felt that day. It was sheer joy and excitement. A smile comes to my face as I reflect on the memory. I was so happy.

The next step was to be baptized or dipped in that liquid grave—i.e the baptism pool. Stories from my cousins about how cold the water was were the highlight leading up to it. My cousins could make you laugh at any story they told.

There were two of us who would be baptized that round. At my church you had to remove the Choir stand seats to get to the water which was located underneath the seats. A big mirror was on the wall so the audience could see you.

We were brought out and escorted over to the water. I was dressed in white linen from head to toe because you couldn't wear your regular clothes. I went first. The Pastor stood on my right side and his assistants on the left. I looked down at them and at the water. The pastor reached out to grab my little hands. I had crissed-crossed my arms across my chest. The deacon to my left had moved to the right of me and placed his hand on the small of my back. The Pastor put his hand on my left shoulder and started praying. I can't recall

17

his exact words but the next thing I knew I was getting dipped. His hand went from my shoulder to my back. His other hand was on my face closing my nostrils and cupping my mouth.

"One for the Father. One for the Son. One for the Holy Ghost."

After being dunked in the cold ass water I heard singing ring out throughout the church. I saw my aunt reach for me. Her eyes were filled with tears.

Back in the Pastor's office, somebody who I don't remember wrapped me in white linen cloth. My mom and the rest of my family were there. I smiled inside. Tears filled my eyes. I guess I was full to the rim. It was the best day of my life and there's a picture to prove it!

I was baptized. I had given my life to Christ and now I could sing in the choir. That's what I truly wanted to do.

Growing up in church was quite entertaining. My cousins went to the same church so I was never bored or lonely.

Church felt like home. I got lots of, "I'm going to whoop if you keep acting stares." There was always family and food. Those were some of the greatest moments in my life. I wouldn't trade them for anything.

Singing in the choir was the bomb.com for me. I was able to lead songs, sing in front of family and the congregation. The benefit of growing up in a small church was that even the people you weren't related to were like family. The majority of the time you didn't know the difference because everybody treated you like kin.

The small Baptist church I attended had amazing singers. My aunt was one of them. I also loved hearing Miss Tina sing and play the piano.

A good time, oh yeah! A mighty, mighty good time!

If she didn't inspire you to sing Mr. Joe did. He could go from Tenor to Soprano with ease. Sister Sybil could blow too. These four rocked out on Sunday mornings. I loved it! All of them touched my life with their singing. I am grateful to have witnessed and experienced such wondrous angels in the flesh...

There was this one particular girl I wanted to sit by at rehearsal. She was a little older but still a "Git" as one of my cousins calls me. I had a school girl crush on her. Now that I'm older and can differentiate what was going on, I know that's what it was. I wanted to be close to her so I could feel the emotions of crushing all over me.

There was this one girl I was crushing in middle school. Of course my silly-self had to go and tell her I liked her. I was so nervous! I told her while we were leaving class. Ha!

I also remember the first girl's boobs my face was in between! That was the coolest shit ever! Several folks saw me do it. I don't know what made me do it. Afterward I denied that fact that I had done it even though an entire audience witnessed the act. I was relaxing in her lap with her boobs on my shoulders. That was really nice....

My first real sexual innuendo happened with a close friend. We were in Middle School—I was in the 8th grade.

Let me back up—I had a boyfriend for a little while but by the 8th grade I was single. I was still interacting with boys but had strong feelings towards girls. I had learned not to pay too much attention to those feelings until I met *her*. The encounter happened while I was over my close friend house. I'd spent the night after a school-sponsored pool party.

We still had on our bathing suits. I was sitting on her bed. She was in front of the mirror modeling her bathing suit and talking to me. I had put my street clothes on over my suit. In the midst of our conversation she said she wanted to see my bathing suit. I proceeded to take my shirt off. I never thought her mounting me and feeling on my breast would come after, "Oh, it's cute." I was stunned, unable to move. She took my hands and put them on her breasts and proceeded to move them around. I moved my hands as she directed me to without uttering a word.

After a few minutes, she got up, went to get sleeping attire and started talking about an unrelated topic like what had just gone down hadn't happened. Later that evening she would do it again. This time she showed me more of her naked skin. Her nipples were dark and lovely. I was happy to oblige and knew exactly what to do when she took my hands and placed them on her bosom.

While the second encounter was brief, she seemed to enjoy it. Afterwards we got ourselves ready for bed. While she went to take a shower, I lay there in shock.

Had that really happened?
Did I like it?

What the hell?

Shit!

I was calm but had no words that could pin point my emotions. I'd just had my first encounter. It was on some *feel me feel you* type of vibe.

When she came back we were both ready for bed. There was a little more talking then it was lights out. I couldn't go to sleep. I was lying next to my close friend, my homie, my bestie, staring up at the ceiling. Her position was with her back facing me. I was still in my thoughts thinking WTF just happened. Finally, after a good long while I started to fall asleep. That's when she grabbed my breast and put my hand on hers once again.

We were new to this, at least I was. It came natural to her. The feelings were so true for me. She knew what she wanted and I followed suit.

Her motions, her body—they felt so good and familiar to me. Caressing went to sucking, sucking to kissing. I couldn't stop even if I'd wanted to. I didn't want to stop.

Even though I was in disbelief of what was happening I proceeded. We hit the ball around for a while but only got to second base. Tired and spent we drifted off the sleep. I woke to hearing her moving around with her family in the living room. My mind immediately went to what had happened only hours ago.

When I saw her she nodded good morning and gave me an *I'm more than your homie now* look. My ass didn't know what to do. That experience with her changed something in me but I put it to the side and moved on.

She and I remained friends but that never happened again. It was a monumental moment in my life. I wouldn't have that type of encounter again until I meet *her* one year later at a church convention. I was in High School.

Chapter 4

Riddle me this
Riddle me that why can't I keep my lips off
your spine?
The perfectness in the arch that's been
created in your back…..

Church was a repetitious tradition in my family. On Sundays it was robotic. Same ole shit different day describes it perfectly. I was still getting those threats about God's punishment if I failed to obey Him. So while sleeping in was the option—I was clear that I had no job, I was still in school and my mom, aunts and grandmother still cooked 95% of my meals. Well, cereal was the 5% I made on my own. Well…maybe spaghetti was another 5%. My brothers still clown me about not learning to cook to cook that spaghetti right to this day.

More childhood memories…I recall the time I had a conversation with my mom through the window. It happened that way because I had come home late several days in a row. She had warned me to not continue coming in the house that late. I was out with my cousins. Getting in trouble with them happened more than it did when I was alone in the act.

I was still known as the "goodie two shoes" of the family. Then there was the time we had decided to take a trip to the next city which, by the way, was only five minutes away by car. We traveled on bikes.

My cousin's bike decided to break down while we were in route. Her handle bars were rotating and pedals malfunctioning. Then someone had the bright idea to take the railroad tracks back home instead of the regular road. We all agreed to that brilliant plan.

Walking along the railroad tracks was like walking in the DESERT! It was hot. I was thirsty. They were thirsty. Jokes were being made. While everyone was walking beside their bicycles another bright idea parted the lips of another one of my cousins. He picked up a nail from the railroad track. It was old and worn by Father Time. He encouraged all of us to retrieve one of the nails as a souvenir.

By the time we got home the street lights were on. I remember going to the bathroom and looking in the mirror. When I took my bandana off my head, part of my face was a different complexion than the other part I started off with that day.

This part of the book takes me back to church. So much of this book takes place on that holy ground. Clearly, church and family were and are an important part of my life.

Sunday's sitting in church became different after meeting *her*. I was supposed to be focusing on the prayer. She made the prayer hard to focus on. My feelings for her reminded me of that Jamie Foxx song *Sex*. Especially that line where he says, "Even when I tried to pray it off, it don't work!" Yes! I can definitely testify to that. She or her that is, was the truth, the whole truth and nothing but the truth. A *three snaps up, three snaps down* type of moment.

She was in my system. It was like I had been programmed by her. Being around her was what I wanted and what I needed. She was my first real love jones and I had it bad. So did she. Our first encounter had been intense. Our lips never left each other. The trip to her seemed like it took months. In between visits we called and wrote each other.

######

My mom and aunt talked as we drove.
I heard them but I didn't know what they were
talking about. I wasn't listening. I was watching
the scenery outside, listening to the car as the
wheels turned on the axel. We were getting closer
to the house, closer to *her* house.

We pulled up and she came outside with a
smile on her face. She was all happy and giddy. I
got out the car with my things while she spoke to
my mother and aunt. After a little small talk, my
mom and aunt said their goodbyes. Then we were
inside. The air was heavy and thick. Our
emotions were on the verge of taking over....

All the telephone conversations, the letters,
now it was time. I could feel her. We had
chemistry, strong chemistry. We entered her room.
She was supposed to be watching her sister. She
was outside playing with her friends. Her mother
was at work. My parents were gone. I positioned
myself on the floor, belly down, facing the TV.
She did the same but she was on her bed. We
watched TV, talked and laughed.

The tension grew even more intense. We
both knew damn well the TV and small talk was a
decoy. We were both fooling ourselves, even if
only for a little while.

"Why are you on the floor?" words that came from her.

"I don't know. I'm comfortable—didn't know if you wanted me on your bed."

The dumbest shit I could have ever said.

She invited me up. I accepted. Still, I sat close to the edge. She was lying at the foot of her bed facing the TV. Her head was slightly turned in my direction. Our silence was powerful. Our chemistry was like electricity. We could have lit up an entire city. I reach out my hand and touched her shoulder. My touch made her quiver.

I removed my hand from her shoulder. Shit was intense! I leaned over and kissed her shoulder while out the corner of my eye, looking to see her reaction. Her eyes closed. She moved her head toward me, let her lips part slightly. I moved back for a few, repeated the last motion, ended my act with a kiss on her cheek planted closely by her mouth.

"Stop teasing me," she said.

I grinned and proceeded to do it again.
Before I could move away she stopped me. She placed her lips upon mine and a deep, sensual,

passionate kisses began. We went from the bed to the wall. THE RUSH! My cup runneth over. The intensity, the delight!

It was real. What we were doing went completely and totally beyond the norm. There wasn't an ounce of reconsideration in my bones. I was in the moment and so was she. Time seemed to stop just for us.

The energy between us wasn't like anything I'd ever experienced. I was hooked immediately. Being with her felt so natural it shocked the shit out of me!

Everything in me was alive. The feelings consumed me just like the Holy Ghost people at church talked about. I was speechless, breathless. That moment would prove unforgettable. And this was just from her kisses. We had yet to get to home base. It was so surreal. I asked myself what kind of movie had we just created?

We went through an emotional roller coaster of feelings because of our religious backgrounds. Afterwards I found myself not sleeping at night. She had tears in her eyes.

I felt so indecisive. The things I'd heard people say about being gay were never positive. I wondered if I'd bought a ticket straight to hell or condemned my soul. Thoughts of Sodom and Gomorra went through my mind.

I had been taught what we were doing was not of God. But when I heard here voice and felt her presence, the words of Jay Z's song came to my mind.

If you go to heaven and I go to hell just sneak out and meet me bring a box of L's

Chapter 5

I remember the times I said things that hurt her. Saying things like, *we can't be together, this isn't right.* I knew—even in my fear—that I wanted her and that she made me happy. I caused her so many tears over the few months I was torn between how I was raised and how she and I being together made perfect sense.

I finally got past it after a conversation with my cousin. I pretty much told her everything. She's younger than me but very wise for her age. She always reminded me of her grandmother, who is my aunt.

I told my cousin, "You know that girl I'm really cool with? We ummmm….we had an encounter. We kissed. More than a friend-kiss type of thing. We also did other stuff. I know it isn't right but I want to be with her. "

The look on her face was priceless. She was shocked.

She asked me if I had prayed about it, told me I could go to hell. But she said if I was happy, she still loved me and wouldn't treat me any different. I was relieved when she said that.

I had been praying like the world was coming to an end. I asked the same questions every time.

Is this right?
Is this supposed to be happening?

I asked God to tell me something. A sense of peace came over me. I'd go to sleep and wake up to her being the first thing on my mind. I called her before I even rolled over to get up and use the bathroom. My face lit up with a big smile upon hearing her voice. That sense of peace remained over me.

I positioned myself so that my pillow was over my face so I could say what I wanted to her without being found out. I lived with my peoples. I was in no rush to say anything to them about what was up.

Even when things became even more legit between she and I, even after months had passed and we were still going strong, I still didn't tell them.

It became difficult to stay on guard. I had become comfortable. Plus, I was really happy. The family knowing what was going on between us became the furthest thing from my mind. I was sure they saw how I responded to her. I was sure they knew that I was always trying to be with her or had just left her. She was the only person I brought to family events. I knew saying she was my "bestie" would only work for a while.

It was true that we started out as friends but what we had and did was way more than what best friends did and had. My heart had already decided but my mind was on a whole different level of confused, mixed love emotions.

Years went by and we were still together. Still disguising it as whatever was at hand to play in any situation. We were still talking to boys--a disguise for me.

Sometimes she said I was bisexual. But I knew what was up. I wasn't really feeling men like I was women.

The day I graduated from high school, I looked out and saw the proud look on my mom and dad's face as I walked across the stage to receive my diploma. My dad gave me two thumbs up. My mom was smiling. I saw my special *her* sitting out there proud as well. Her face was full of love. She was in love with me. Still. Three years and some change later. Only a few knew anything about us. I called them the, "faithful few."

I was preparing to go to college. My first choice was out of state. My second choice was Florida A&M. Third, Bethune. I also considered going to college somewhere in Orlando.

My moms approached me with the possibility of going to a two-year college then leaving for a four year college. Finances were her concern. I was kind of cool with that option because she had been working hard for us for a long time. I didn't want to make anything more difficult for her. Going to school out of state was my initial plan but staying in-state wasn't a bad idea either.

The day I received my acceptance letter from FAMU I ran all the way to my aunt's house to share the news while calling my mother. That was one of the happiest days of my life! Several people from my area were going there. I was going to be in the music program and march in the hundred. That was the reason I applied. I called my girlfriend immediately after talking with my mom.

She was excited for me—probably happier than I was. I shared everything with her.

My last time seeing her was bittersweet. We reflected over the ups and downs we shared. So many memorable moments and now we were about to be apart.

There were tears in her eyes. She cared about me so much. This was the woman who had looked all over to get answers to why we couldn't be. She was so determined.

My first few months at school I was scared and nervous. I played like I wasn't though. I was the only person in the dorm until school officially started at pre drill. I was learning what it took to be the best of the best.

Once school started my friends I went to high school with arrived. The fun began. Basement crew--what it do! We established a line that became a trademark to all of us who became close friends in the basement of Wheatley dorms.

I stayed in *Paddy Foote*. I was a *P-Foot Solider* (if you attended or are attending FAMU you're familiar with the term). I met and am still friends with other brilliant, successful Black women who lived there.

I had my first college crush on a cutie with long black hair. She was short and you could tell she was mixed with something. I was definitely into her but I had a lady back at home who could tell if I changed my toothbrush. She knew me just that well. Ugh! At times I didn't like that so much.

She could be emotional—so telling her the truth seemed to make her cry just as much as someone who told lies all the time. I hurt her the most when I would be indecisive or make dumb ass decisions which led me to question what the fuck I was doing immediately afterwards. This caused tension between us even though we were still trying to play the "we're just friends" roles. We both knew it was more.

I couldn't hide it anymore. It showed all over me. I tried to win her heart back from the hurt I caused her. It seemed like nothing would help.

I started crushing on other college girls even though I still called myself, "talking to guys." Guys were few and far in between but I continued going through the motions. The guys I encountered became my friends nothing more.

I remember one day I was on the phone with my mom, walking back to the apartment her and I shared. I used to call my mom every day in college just to hear her voice. We lived near the Alpha house around this time.

Those distinguished Black Alpha men could be handsome. I happened to see one outside that day with his shirt off (of course). He was light-skinned, had a nice fade, was in shape (at least from a distance).

On the phone, walking from class, in a playful voice I said, "Ma, this Alpha guy looks good girl."

My mother said, so smoothly might I add, that, "She doesn't think I really like guys."

My heart dropped to my foot. I stopped immediately in my tracks.

My mom had asked me before if I liked girls. Of course I denied the fact that I wasn't into women and brushed it off like she'd lost her mind when in fact she was hitting the nail right on the head.

She was aware I'd had sex with a guy but she didn't know it had been a long while since that happened. And in that secret place in my mind I wasn't looking to do it again.

I answered, "Ma! Are you serious?"

She said, "What? I'm just saying"

"Nah, ma, I'm good."

I wasn't ready to tell myself or my mother the truth. By this time, me and my special HER were living together. She ended up coming to FAMU as well.

Things were rough for a while. I mean every time the sun came up it was just rough. My classes were becoming overwhelming. Trying to take care of her, work and attend school was a challenge. Hospital visits were frequent. I was the only family she had.

My special friend and I had our good days and our bad. She still interacted with guys. I didn't. We eventually broke up. I was a little upset knowing I was the one she came home to even though we weren't together. I still wanted to be with HER. I realized part of the reason I was wanted to be with her was out of guilt from the things I'd done before. I was constantly apologizing to her, often for no reason, as we continued our on and off interactions. I guess it was to stroke her ego. There are some life lessons and experiences with her with her that I'll never forget. Later, I realized they were for my good.

It was never to harm me but to make me grow—a growth I truly needed.

#####

My last encounter with a man made the lessons with my special her very clear. He was marriage material, very ambitious and quite handsome. Let me add that years had passed since the young lady and I were a couple but we still fooled around on and off. We also lived together like that helped any. She had a boyfriend! Not the best situation. He was a gentleman, well dressed with simplicity and style. His Pants hanging too far below his waist wasn't his thing. He was well groomed, had a job and in college close to finishing his degree. TOO GOOD TO BE DAMN TRUE!

I can't recall how I exactly met him.... Hold on, yes I do! I was a security officer at the time. That night I was working in the complex he lived in. HER and I were still living together. We had moved to a different location on the other side of campus. She and I would stay on the phone until she fell asleep even though we weren't in a relationship. At the time, we were each talking to a couple of dudes.

We were at liberty to see who we wanted, when we wanted but still the connection we had. When I got off work, it was her bed I got into without a second thought. I lay beside her like we were the married couple we'd been playing for years.

Seeing others while still playing house— that's exactly how your feelings get tangled all up in a bunch. One person is cool with seeing others while the other pretends like the shit is ok. We were longing to rekindle what once was but knowing deep inside it would never happen again.

The new male friend said he had seen me around. We had small talk before he headed up to his room. He seemed cool and I liked his style. He dressed the way I would've liked to see all men dress.

Now back to what I was saying, his approach was cool calm and collected. We exchanged numbers and of course I told her about it.

Now this is what was interesting about what was going on. She was cool with me talking to guys but a girl--HELL NAW! This was because of a promise we made to each other when we were younger—to not be with another woman after us just men. Not the best promise I could have made to someone. Neither ethical or realistic...

She encouraged my talking to him. I did as she encouraged. Time went by. He and I were still talking. He was real cool and I genuinely liked him and cared about him.

Still I longed for her and what we *used* to have. Trying to be her friend but fighting back the hurt of seeing her with someone else. Some of the guys she went out with noticed my actions with her when we were together. They knew something was up.

When the friends who knew we had something going on were around she'd act different towards me. If it was just us or people who were close to me, she would give me affection. But that was rare.

We moved into a new place again. She never wanted to stay anywhere too long. It seemed like once we really settled in, she was ready to move. Telling her no was not something she accepted. She'd dismiss it like a fly. She always found a way to get what she wanted.

Only in the secret of my room did I expose my truths. I was frustrated over just losing my job right before we moved, dealing with being in a new place and recently joining a new church. She'd gotten mad at me for joining without her. She went back with the dude she dated in high school who was now living with us.

All of this change in a matter of a few short months.

I found a job delivering newspapers. She would go with me on my routes sometimes. I wasn't sure if she was concerned about my safety or didn't want to be at the house because they had gotten into it. She was still running to me when shit "got real" and I still allowed it. I had wishful thinking that she would just stay with me but once I made everything better she'd grab her stilettos, fancy purse, earrings, make up and go back to the dame shit.

HE would visit, not too frequent. He had work and school.

He and I made out once. He was on the way out. His arousal was apparent as was his strength. Our first date was at Lake Ella. We walked, talked and held hands. She was excited for me but it was evident in her actions that she still had feelings for me as well.

She knew I wanted to make love to her. And I knew she wanted to make love to me. Her hugs spoke the truth of her attraction for me as she would linger from the embrace. It was only a matter of time before we had sex again for the millionth time. Our chemistry stayed intact while I was living with her and the high school jock. I was pissed!

I wasn't feeling our current situation. I distanced myself as much as possible and started exercising to get my mind off things.

I still didn't tell *Him* who I now call, *The Gentleman* this about us. I sensed he could tell there was something but I paid his possible assumptions no attention.

At the time the old but new "BF" didn't understand my actions. I was still polite when I wanted to be but I was angry inside. I was trying to get over but it was proving more difficult than I anticipated.

The first night I stayed with *The Gentleman* she tried not to show wasn't too keen on it. Her questions and concerns were centered on whether he and I were going to have sex. My answer was no, I didn't think we were. But if it happened it happened. I was enjoying someone else's company it wasn't like she had stopped having sex with other people for me.

I saw the hurt in her eyes as I left with *The Gentleman.* I was nervous at the thought of having sex with him. She had put it on my mind when she brought it up prior to our leaving the house. When we arrived at his house, I met his roommate. We chilled for a while, talked, watched a little TV then shower time came. I was a bit more relaxed when I went to take my shower but I was thinking about her. I looked at myself in his bathroom and barely recognizing who I was. I continued on because that's what I had learned to do.

I lay there thinking in his bed as he showered. I glanced at the TV from time to time then back at the ceiling. I knew better days were approaching. I could feel it. Though inside I was hurting, on the outside I wore a smile on my face. I knew my happiness inspired others so I didn't show the truth. Only my walls and two of my close friends knew how I really felt.

He entered the room, shirt off, shorts on. He was semi fit—he played soccer in his free time. He used to body build when he was younger and I could tell. His skin was the color of chocolate. He had been educated both in school and out. He got in bed with me and began small talk. The look in his eyes, the kisses he laid on my lips—all implied he wanted more though it was not rushed.

I engaged with him.

He was on the side of me, then he was on top of me then below my waist line. His touch was different from that of a woman's touch but I allowed it. In my thoughts I wasn't sure what to make of it. The condom, the slow entrance—the very, very slow entrance—penetration was not my thing.

It had been years and I mean years, since I had been with a man. Fortunately, he was concerned and gentle with me. The only light in the room was coming from his laptop. He had some nice music playing. We weren't even good into it before she came to my mind. My tears began a conversation with my eyes. I was feeling some type of way—like I had done an injustice. I felt it through my entire body.

What was I doing?

There were more tears. I knew he felt my pain. He asked me if something was wrong. The

"No" of a lie I told him but he could definitely tell something was not right. I had my face turned away from him.

He stopped, asked me again if I was ok. I said nothing, still looking away.
I couldn't go through with it.

The next morning, we tried it again. He got his very quickly but still no feeling from me. She called seem immediately afterwards.

She started the conversation with a "Hi," asked me how things went and did I have sex with him. Me answering truthfully, her saying she knew it. Me getting upset telling her we didn't finish but tried again. Her asking why and honestly, me not knowing why the hell I went through the motions again.

In a way I was getting back at her. The sex sounds I'd heard her make while being in the same house. Her seeming to not give two fucks about me being there at all. The shit had me angry and hurting me at the same time. I distanced myself from him, tried to figure out what the hell I was doing with myself.

I still talked to him. Made everything seem alright when it wasn't.

She finally told the "old but new high school boyfriend" about her and I. Something he already knew but she now confirmed. That didn't help their relationship at all. He was already having insecurity issues about things that happened before them with other guys. They started arguing more frequently. Good days happened less. I was getting better at moving forward from everything, getting better at accepting who I was for real. Going to church was even helping. I was still going back and forth in my mind pretty strong but let a fine woman walk by me. Oh yeah, that definitely caught my eye and took my mind off of it all. Sigh, the art of a woman....

If you've ever heard the phrase, "beating a dead horse," you understand where I was at that point. I knew even though he was dead, his spirit was very much alive. My answer came to me one night at a youth conference..... The Alter Call.

Chapter 6

I still care about him til' this day but being with him wouldn't have been the best move. Our conversations were good, we made each other laugh and he cared for me. He helped so much when I needed him. He fed me when I was hungry, visited me when I hit a tree riding a bicycle one night. We will always bid each other well. But I really needed to accept that there was not and never would be a him and I.

I tried to be involved with him romantically but the truth about me was becoming more obvious in my own eyes when I looked in the mirror. He and I weren't around each other often and my awakening was occurring. I found myself seeking, reading. I read the, *Living the Wisdom of the Tao* by Dr. Wayne Dyer. This book gave me a whole new perspective.

I was rooming with a friend and she had moved back home. We weren't talking much at all. The space we were taking now was needed years ago. We were growing apart drastically and we were still trying to hold on to bits and pieces of what use to be and not fully moving forward because of it.

My male friend and I remained in contact even after the many extreme moments she and I had. In fact, we became great friends. If I needed to talk, he not only gave me advice and he didn't judge me.

I never told my male friend what was going on with me and her. I never told him the truth about me. While reading Dr. Wayne Dyer's book, I began to see things differently and allowed the changed that was occurring to happen. I knew all along that the truth was what I needed but I fought it down to the last breath.

I was seeking God in a way I never had before. I read the bible time after time, searching for peace and understanding. The temporary fix I was getting wasn't enough.

I couldn't breathe in that energy any longer. I was uncomfortable all the way down to my spirit. Thinking about it now, so much self-growth had occurred. Dr. Wayne Dyer's version of the Tao helped tremendously along with attending church at times and reading the bible.

I wasn't reading the bible so much when I was reading the *The Tao.* Both books taught the importance of *knowing thyself.* I started to pick up on things I hadn't picked up on before. Peace was all over me and in *her* presence I wanted to stay. I began to get to know her (peace) the summer prior to me rooming with my homeboy.

Earlier in my story I mentioned me hitting a tree. Yes, it happened. Along with me losing both my jobs in the same day.

Getting in a car accident a few weeks later, I wasn't paying attention to what I was doing. My brush was more important to me than looking at the road.

That and not being able to find a place to live after my lease as up. Then having to live at the church for a week. Then living in Alabama for a week or two. Then going back to Tally (Tallahassee) with a woman who blessed me by letting me stay at her place until I got back on my feet. You would have thought I'd move back home. Those doors were and will always be open but I couldn't it wasn't in me to take that route at the time.

With all that had gone on that summer I was at peace. I finally understood and knew what it meant to have "peace that surpassed all understanding." No one understood how I could be so calm in the midst of so much turmoil. At first I didn't understand it but as the events occurred I began to understand how love really works. I knew God at an entirely different level then I had ever known before.

This time when I looked in the mirror it wasn't me I just saw anymore, I could see God. I had an understanding about myself that I knew without a doubt was true to who I was and who I am now. He's really going to make some woman glad she waited on a good man, a very happy woman. Namaste. Waking up—finally being honest with myself.

Communication with her had dwelled down to damn near zero. That "Be a friend over it all" crap was the pits and didn't work at all. The time away from her helped me grow to where I needed to be. Leading me to not to be angry with her for doing what I knew deep inside she would do. Having a mature, *finally* honest conversation with God and loving me for who I truly was....

The night of the youth conference was a major turning point in my life.

I grew up in church so being active in a position was normal for me. I was on post doing what I knew from the younger years to do--giving my time to God. It's amazing how some thing's just stick with you.

Youth conferences are fun. This one ran from Friday to Sunday. Sunday was when the big shift took place. That would be the last conversation I had with God about my sexuality. I was seeing life in a whole new light and it was simply amazing. The universe and all its beauty. I felt so loved by its wonders and was loving myself even more.

Everyone was enjoying themselves. The performances were exciting and engaging. Everything from the beginning sessions leading up to the main speaker—we were having a blast. It was Sunday, while looking at myself though the eyes of God, that I was given what I had been asking for for so long.

Sunday morning started off the same but with the youth in charge of the services. Services began with praise and worship, the reading of the Word and prayer. The different selections continued from there with each group who came up to perform. I was on my post engaged in the service.

Things calmed down a bit but the energy was still high. It was time for the main speaker to come up. It wasn't a guest that came up to speak that day.

The speaker was a member, one of the Elders at the church. He was introduced before the last selection of the Youth Choir. Typically before we started the lesson or speech, we began with a prayer. Everyone was already standing when he began the prayer. This was done to acknowledge and respect the anointing on his life, church edict. He hit on so many different topics young adults deal with on their journey to becoming adults.

Peer pressure, sex, drugs, low self-esteem and more and I mean he was getting it!

I'd always noticed when this particular Elder was speaking how his enthusiasm was matched from sound to movement. He walked from corner to corner of the stage, engaging the congregation that sat before him, he owned it.

Conformation that he was on his game came in form of *Amens* and *You Better Say It* that were being tossed through the air like jump balls from different sides of the church. He was working his way to a powerful close. He was still hitting some touchy topics. Fornication flew on the list. I bet you can guess exactly which one I'm about to name next....

Homosexuality.

Look at you all smart and what not...lol.

He began to make his appeal to the congregation but more importantly to the youth. After all, this conference was for us and about us. At this point and time in the service, his level was on an eight. I was paying attention. Most of my attention was on the atmosphere in the room though. How the energy had filled the place.

He asked that those who could speak in their heavenly language, in *tongues* that is, to begin to do so. Then he invited youth to come up who were dealing with the topics he named so he could pray for them.

The first topic he named was homosexuality.

There was hesitation in the air and slight discomfort. You could see the stillness that came over the room and the thoughts that filled everyone's mind. It seemed surreal. There in the middle of all it. I was. The speaker went on to ask those who felt the need to come up to come.

I saw the first person jump up quick and go up front. Interestingly enough, it was a person who I did wonder about on occasion. I turned away and closed my eyes and continued in my heavenly language. I lost all sense of my surroundings. My awareness of myself heightened times ten. I was very present with who I was. While in such a pure moment, I proceeded to ask God should I go up there.

"God, we've been having this conversation for a long time. Should I go?"

Expecting a yes or no answer, my question was answered with a question. The words flowed and rung in my ears in a way I'd never felt before or heard.
"Do you think you should go?"

Taken back by the question that came, an immediate no with surety but nervousness came to my mind.

Wow I thought to myself.

I was sure because damn, it was the truth. My truth. The nervousness because damn it was the truth, my truth. I answered confidently and boldly to God and myself.

In my secret place, which is the place of full awareness of who I am, who I have been all my life, I had my answer.

I didn't see who all went up only the first person. I never looked back in that moment I had with God. I also reflected over how far I'd come. I reflected too on how some folks had never treated me different and how some kept their distance. I thought about how for so long I denied who I was to fit in with what I knew.

A comfort zone, trapped in a box finding out truths I didn't see right in front of me about myself. All because of the standards of being a church girl. I loved church. I loved going to church. I loved the people who inspired me there. It's where I learned so much. Its where I got into the process of finding the REAL me.

Church is where if I can't find one of the people I love, I know to go there every time. Amazing isn't it? Even right now as I'm writing I can understand why my aunt told me about an important moment in my life as a child. Her first time telling me this was one late night on the phone. She called around three something in the morning. I was half sleep, wondering why she was calling that time of night.

She said when I was about three years old I told her I was a boy. She told me exactly how I said it. She informed me again in person at one of our family gathering. I don't deny that I didn't say it.

I believe I knew who I was at three. After she told me of that moment she looked at me with love and genuineness and said, "Be who you are."

I could do nothing but smile and say yes ma'am as I continued to show her the women whom I felt had potential in my life. She even asked about the former girl who was in my life.

I said, "I've been single for a while now auntie you need to catch up."

I remember having a laugh-out-loud moment in my head as I addressed her questions.
I was glad to even be having that conversation with her, knowing that she loved me unconditionally. That it was alright that I'm a woman who loves women and that the journey to myself was worth every step.

Kourtney Shavon Carter spends her time inspiring young women and men to be successful, pursuing higher education and taking part in empowerment sessions for budding entrepreneurs.

About Kourtney

Kourtney S. Carter was born and raised in Lake Wales, FL. Her first love was music. She first discovered it growing up in a musical family, where singing happened quite often. In her early years she continued to follow her love for music by being in a band, singing and playing instruments in church. While growing up in church she became a role model and mentor to her peers and youth in her community. She also participated in Big Brothers Big Sisters while in high school among other volunteer activities with her church and school in her community.

Kourtney also had a love for basketball. She played basketball along with music until her senior year in high school where she became one of the first African American female drum majors at Lake Wales High School in 2006!

Kourtney pursued her college education at Florida A&M University. While in pursuit of her degree Kourtney wrote songs and poems in her spare time and worked a full time job as well. She took time off from school to discover who she truly was. In this quest for self growth, Kourtney was lead to write a book! Initially, she had considered book writing later in life once she had acquired her Ph. D. However, Kourtney was lead different direction and went forth with what she was lead to do... instead of being led to just become an author, Kourtney has always felt lead to become more of herself.

Dreams of mentoring and traveling the world are still very much alive in her heart. Kourtney learned that it's important to the entire world to follow your dreams of living the way you desire. In doing so, you allow others around you to project their greatness as well. Ms. Carter is currently preparing to finish up here bachelor degree at Florida A&M University.

About Glover Lane Press

Thank you so much for purchasing this one of a kind memoir by Kourtney Carter

I am truly excited about our role in publishing this inspirational work.

If you enjoyed reading "When a Woman Loves a Woman", please visit our website for our new, featured and upcoming publications.

Azaan Kamau started Glover Lane Press in the summer of 2000 to give a voice to poets, journalists, and writers worldwide. Azaan and Glover Lane Press have helped countless individuals publish and distribute media in print and in digital formats.

As a woman, one of Azaan's publishing goals is to focus on marginalized or over-looked communities of writers, poets, artist, and photographers. Azaan feels everyone has a story that must be heard or recorded. Another important goal is to use the proceeds from sales of Azaan's books to improve the lives of people around the world. Azaan's books and her companies will feed the hungry, house the homeless, heal the sick, educate and eradicate disease, etc!

Thank you again for your purchase.

www.gloverlanepress.webs.com

www.ingramcontent.com/pod-product-compliance
Lightning Source LLC
Chambersburg PA
CBHW030030290326
41934CB00005B/559